On July I, 1863, the First Minnesota Infantry Regiment set up camp just outside the small town of Gettysburg, Pennsylvania.

Among the soldiers were two brothers, Patrick and Isaac Taylor. In his journal that night, Patrick wrote: "Made coffee, built barricade of fence rails, and lay down to sleep. My brother and I talk of the expected battle tomorrow."

It would be one of the last conversations the brothers ever had.

Patrick (left) and Isaac Taylor

On July 2, the Taylor brothers took part in a furious attack on a Confederate brigade. Their regiment was greatly outnumbered, and in ten minutes, it lost 215 of its 262 men.

Isaac was killed during the charge, and Patrick buried his brother on the battlefield. "I was the only one to weep at his grave," he wrote in his journal a few days later.

Isaac Taylor was one of more than 7,500 soldiers who died during the three-day Battle of Gettysburg.

Patrick and Isaac Taylor were in the First Minnesota Infantry Regiment, part of the Union Army. Here, the regiment makes its doomed charge against a Confederate brigade.

Photographs © 2010: **age fotostock/Dennis MacDonald:** 21; **Alamy Images/ Chris Pondy:** 20 left; **AP Images/Carolyn Kaster:** 28, 29; **Art Resource, NY:** 33 top, 53 top (The New York Public Library), 55 top; **Bridgeman Art Library International Ltd., London/New York/Private Collection:** 54; **Center for Civil War Photography, NPS/Gettysburg National Military Park:** 1; **Corbis Images:** 44, 45, 55 bottom (Bettmann), 17 bottom (Tria Giovan), 9 bottom (Medford Historical Society Collection), 48 (Richard T. Nowitz), 12 left (The Corcoran Gallery of Art), 16, 34, 50; **DK Images/Dave King:** 24 bottom; **Getty Images:** 30 (Michael Melford), back cover, 51 top (MPI), 41 (Stock Montage), 7 bottom left (Time & Life Pictures); **Gettysburg National Military Park/NPS/from** *Battles and Leaders of the Civil War:* 32; **iStockphoto/BDPhoto:** 35; **Library of Congress, Prints and Photographs Division:** 33 bottom (Brady-Handy Photograph Collection), 5, 10 bottom, 11 bottom, 12 right, 13 bottom, 40 (Alexander Gardner), 13 top (Gladstone Collection), 27, 52 (Timothy H. O'Sullivan), cover (Timothy H. O'Sullivan, hand-tinted by Red Herring), 31 (F.E. Wright, painting by H.A. Ogden), 47 bottom, 53 bottom; **Military and Historical Image Bank/www.historicalimagebank.com:** 2, 3, 14, 15, 22, 38 (Don Troiani), 7 bottom right, 7 top, 11 top, 20 center, 20 right, 39, 49, 51 center; **National Archives and Records Administration:** 47 top (Brady National Photographic Art Gallery, 111-B-17), 18, 19 (Timothy H. O'Sullivan, 165-SB-35), 42, 43 (Timothy H. O'Sullivan, 165-SB-42); **National Museum of Health and Medicine/ Armed Forces Institute of Pathology/NCP 3675:** 51 bottom; **Paths of History Art Publisher/painting by Ron Lesser/www.ronlesser.com:** 24 top, 25; **The Granger Collection, New York:** 9 top, 10 top, 17 top; **Tillie Pierce House:** 46; **Valentine Richmond History Center:** 8; **www.sonofthesouth.net:** 36.

Maps by David Lindroth, Inc.

Book design: Red Herring Design/NYC

Library of Congress Cataloging-in-Publication Data
Johnson, Jennifer, 1965–
Gettysburg : the bloodiest battle of the Civil War / Jennifer Johnson.
p. cm. — (24/7 goes to war)
Includes bibliographical references and index.
ISBN-13: 978-0-531-25528-5 (lib. bdg.) 978-0-531-25453-0 (pbk.)
ISBN-10: 0-531-25528-X (lib. bdg.) 0-531-25453-4 (pbk.)
1. Gettysburg, Battle of, Gettysburg, Pa., 1863—Juvenile literature.
I. Title.
E475.53.J65 2010
973.7'349—dc22
2009016545

1 2 3 4 5 6 7 8 9 10 R 19 18 17 16 15 14 13 12 11 10 09

GETTYSBURG

The Bloodiest Battle of the Civil War

JENNIFER JOHNSON

Franklin Watts®
An Imprint of Scholastic Inc.

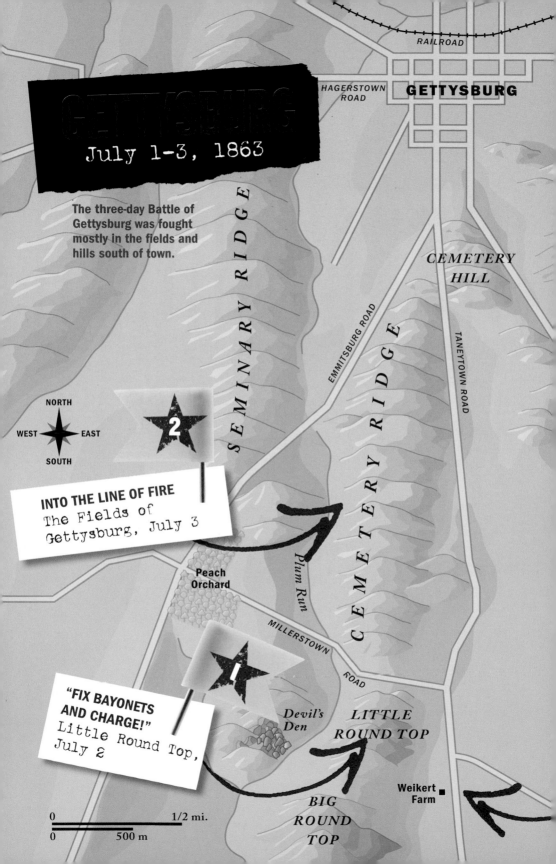

RAILROAD

HAGERSTOWN
ROAD

GETTYSBURG

CEMETERY
HILL

GETTYSBURG
July 1-3, 1863

The three-day Battle of
Gettysburg was fought
mostly in the fields and
hills south of town.

S E M I N A R Y   R I D G E

EMMITSBURG ROAD

TANEYTOWN ROAD

C E M E T E R Y   R I D G E

NORTH

WEST — EAST

SOUTH

2

INTO THE LINE OF FIRE
The Fields of
Gettysburg, July 3

Peach
Orchard

Plum Run

MILLERSTOWN
ROAD

1

**"FIX BAYONETS
AND CHARGE!"**
Little Round Top,
July 2

Devil's
Den

LITTLE
ROUND TOP

Weikert
Farm

BIG
ROUND
TOP

0 — 1/2 mi.
0 — 500 m

★ **3**

"THE REBELS ARE COMING!"
The Weikert Farm,
July 1-3

Confederate soldiers
from Virginia

A NATION DIVIDED

"**W**ar! . . . I cannot study. I cannot sleep, and I don't know as I can write." Those were the thoughts of an Ohio college student in April 1861. From Georgia to Vermont, the news was out: A U.S. fort in South Carolina had fallen to southern troops. The American Civil War had begun.

The war had been sparked by a conflict that had smoldered for decades: the debate over slavery. Four million black people were enslaved in the South—a third of the region's population. Their labor kept the economies of the 15 slave-holding states going. As the United States expanded westward, most southern whites wanted slavery to expand with it. Many northerners were determined to stop it in its tracks.

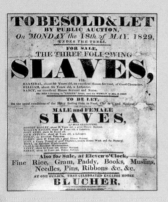

A poster from 1829 announcing the sale of enslaved people

The conflict came to a head on November 6, 1860, when Abraham Lincoln was elected president. Lincoln had once declared, "I believe this government cannot endure permanently half slave and half free." White southerners worried that he was about to make the country entirely free.

On December 20, South Carolina seceded, or broke away, from the Union. Other states soon followed. In February 1861, they formed their own nation: the Confederate States of America. Six thousand South Carolina militiamen took up positions around Fort Sumter, and the stage was set for the opening shots of the war.

A Union sergeant of the 7th New York State Militia in 1861

9

After a day and a half of intense shelling, U.S. soldiers at Fort Sumter surrendered to the Confederate army. There was no denying it now: The nation was at war with itself.

Lincoln called for 75,000 men to join the Union army and stop the Rebels from the South. These volunteers were to serve for 90 days, long enough—most people thought—to bring an end to the war.

The Union army hoped to sign up 30,000 soldiers at this recruiting office in New York City.

Young men flooded military recruiting centers in both North and South, eager to get in on the action before the fighting stopped. "All fun and frolic," said a jubilant private from Mississippi.

That was the mood on July 21, when hundreds of civilians packed picnic baskets and followed the Union army south from Washington, D.C., hoping to see the first big battle of the war.

Near a creek called Bull Run, they got their wish. But when the Confederates attacked, the poorly trained Union soldiers—and the picnickers—ran for their lives. Staggering back to Washington, one Union soldier told a reporter, "I'm going home. I've had enough fighting to last my lifetime."

President Lincoln (in top hat) faces off with General McClellan, commander of the Union's Army of the Potomac.

No Easy Victory

Northerners were shocked by the defeat at Bull Run. They outnumbered southerners five to one. They had better weapons and more factories than the agricultural South.

This canteen was left behind at Bull Run.

Still, it was becoming clear that victory would not come easily. Lincoln called for hundreds of thousands more volunteers, this time asking them to enlist for three years.

Lincoln's top general, George McClellan, planned an elaborate strategy to capture the Confederate capital of Richmond, Virginia. But months slipped by without McClellan taking any action. Even as General Ulysses S. Grant led Union forces to victories in Kentucky and Tennessee, McClellan stalled. In January 1862, a frustrated Lincoln told an adviser, "If McClellan does not want to use the Army, I would like to borrow it for a time."

In the summer of 1862, McClellan finally made his move in Virginia, marching to within ten miles of Richmond. But with a force half of the size of McClellan's, General Robert E. Lee whipped the Yankees—as southerners often called them—into retreat.

In September, Lee pressed his advantage, launching a bold invasion of the North. He was stopped along Antietam Creek in Maryland. It would be the bloodiest day of the war, leaving 23,000 soldiers dead or wounded. The next day, Lee's army limped back to Virginia.

With a victory in hand, Lincoln made a historic announcement. If the Confederate states refused to return to the Union by the end of the year, he declared, all their slaves "shall be then, thenceforward, and forever free." The Confederates ignored him, and on January 1, 1863, Lincoln signed his Emancipation Proclamation.

Marching to Gettysburg

By the summer of 1863, both North and South were worn out from two years of brutal fighting. Lee had repelled yet another Union attack in Virginia, but his soldiers were running low on supplies.

The corpses of Confederate soldiers killed during the Battle of Antietam. The Civil War was one of the first wars to be photographed.

Confederate General Robert E. Lee

With his back against the wall, General Lee made a desperate move. He launched another invasion of the North.

In June, Lee's troops marched into Pennsylvania, seizing food and supplies as they went. The new Union commander, General George Gordon Meade, shadowed the Confederates to the east. As July neared, the two great armies converged on the small town of Gettysburg for what would be the biggest showdown of the war.

In the North, less than one percent of the population was black. But by 1865, African Americans made up nearly ten percent of the Union army.

July 2:

"FIX BAYONETS AND C

On July 2, the second day of fighting, the battle raged in the fields and hills south of Gettysburg. Here, Colonel Strong Vincent (standing at right) and his Union troops repel a Confederate attack.

"CHARGE!"

Colonel Chamberlain's men were down to their last bullets. How could they hold off another Confederate assault?

Joshua Lawrence Chamberlain was dozing as he walked. A year in the infantry had taught the colonel to sleep on his feet—even at high noon on a warm summer day.

Less than two years before, Chamberlain had been a college professor in Maine. Then war broke out and Chamberlain joined the Union army. Soon he was made head of a regiment, the 20th Maine. Chamberlain's men had fought with distinction in many battles in the South. Now, Chamberlain was leading them north into Pennsylvania.

WORN AND WEARY

The 20th Maine was part of the Union's largest army—the Army of the Potomac. Led by General Gordon Meade, the 95,000-man force was pursuing Confederate General Robert E. Lee.

Lee had led his Army of Northern Virginia into Pennsylvania, hoping to win a major battle in the North. He and Confederate President Jefferson Davis believed that a victory on Union soil would force President Lincoln to end the war and recognize the Confederacy as a separate nation.

Chamberlain was eager to fight to keep his country united. But he feared his troops were growing too weak for battle. Once, the 20th Maine had been 1,000 men strong. Now, only 386 men remained.

Most of the casualties

Colonel Joshua Lawrence Chamberlain

Soldiers at a Union army camp pose for a photograph.

had been felled by illness, not bullets. Many of the remaining troops were in poor health, too. Battered and bone-weary, they had been marching for four days in humid June weather.

When the troops finally entered Pennsylvania, they were greeted by grateful citizens who had lined up to cheer for them and bring them water. The warm welcome raised the soldiers' spirits.

A Union soldier was issued two identical shoes. Over time, the shoes took the shape of the soldier's left and right feet.

Near midnight on July 1, the regiment finally reached the outskirts of Gettysburg. Union and Confederate troops had clashed there earlier that day, and a battle had begun.

Tomorrow, the men of 20th Maine would join the fight. But now, dead tired, they curled up on the hard ground and fell asleep.

Holding the High Ground

The blare of bugles woke the men early the next morning.

Soon the regiment was marching again under a hot sun. As they headed toward the battlefield, they passed wagons filled with wounded and dead soldiers. They could tell that the previous day's fighting had been bloody.

On July 1, the Army of the Potomac had taken a beating. But by day's end, Union troops held the high ground—Culp's Hill, Cemetery Hill, and Cemetery Ridge. Cemetery Ridge was two miles long and ended at a hill called Little Round Top.

Holding the high ground put the Yankees in a strong defensive position. The hills and ridge provided many well-protected spots to set up cannons and other artillery. And the Rebels would have to attack uphill—a serious disadvantage.

Now, General Meade and his troops were waiting for General Lee and the Confederates to make their next move. Chamberlain and his men sat in a field, waiting nervously.

Suddenly, at four o'clock, Rebel cannons erupted with a deafening roar. Lee's attack had finally begun.

As the sounds of battle grew more intense, Chamberlain's commander, Colonel Strong Vincent, rode up. He had just received orders to take the 20th Maine and three other regiments to Little Round Top. They were to defend the hill against any attack.

One of Meade's generals had disobeyed orders and left the hill undefended. Now Confederate troops were headed right for it. If they took Little Round Top, they could sweep around the Union line and attack it from behind. The entire Army of the Potomac—all 95,000 troops—would be threatened.

The battle—and possibly the war—could be lost right there.

The End of the Line

As shells exploded around them, Chamberlain and his men scrambled up Little Round Top.

When they reached the summit, they could see the battle raging in the woods and fields below. They had arrived just in time. Several Rebel regiments were rushing toward the hill.

Gettysburg after the battle. The wounded were cared for in the hospital tents to the right.

NEW AND IMPROVED

MUZZLE: Ammunition was loaded through the muzzle.

RAMROD: Soldiers used this to shove ammo down the barrel of the gun.

The Springfield Model 1861, the most widely used gun during the Civil War, was more accurate—and more deadly—than its predecessors. At the beginning of the Civil War, both armies were using smoothbore muskets that fired accurately only to about 80 yards. Later, most troops switched to rifles—guns with spiraled grooves inside their barrels. The grooves made the bullets spin as they left the gun, which made them fly farther and hit harder.

Now soldiers could hit targets up to 400 yards away. That made frontal attacks much more dangerous. Still, many field commanders continued to order head-on charges, resulting in heavy casualties.

BARREL: The barrel was rifled—cut with a spiral groove.

BAYONET: This long blade could be attached to the end of the gun. Bayonets were used in close fighting.

STATS: The rifle was nearly five feet long and weighed nine pounds.

REAR SIGHT: For taking aim

TRIGGER: When pulled, it released the hammer and discharged the gun.

MINIE BALL: These heavy lead bullets shattered bones beyond repair, resulting in amputated limbs.

HAMMER: When a soldier pulled the trigger, the hammer snapped forward and struck a small explosive. The explosion ignited the gunpowder inside the barrel, sending the bullet out of the gun.

SHOULDER STOCK: A soldier held the stock against his shoulder as he fired.

Chamberlain and his men positioned themselves just below the summit of Little Round Top (shown here) to oppose the Confederate charge.

Vincent quickly positioned his four regiments—1,300 men in all—along the south side of Little Round Top, just below the summit. He placed Chamberlain's 20th Maine at the far left of the Union position—at the very end of the line.

"I place you here," he said to Chamberlain. "This is the left of the Union line. You are to hold this ground at all costs."

DEFENDING THE HILL

Chamberlain and his troops began digging in—piling up rocks to form a long, low wall they could crouch behind as they fired at advancing Confederate soldiers.

Within minutes, the men heard a blood-curdling shriek. It was the Rebel Yell—the war cry of Confederate soldiers on the attack. The battle-hardened 15th Alabama Regiment, under the command of Colonel William C. Oates, was charging up the hill.

Chamberlain ordered his troops to open fire. Bullets ripped through leaves and zinged off rocks. Dozens of Rebel soldiers fell. Through clouds of rifle smoke, Chamberlain saw the Alabamians retreat.

But the Rebels quickly launched another attack. And once again, the 20th Maine pushed them back. As Colonel Oates said later, "The fire was so destructive that my line wavered like a man trying to walk against a strong wind."

Chamberlain scrambled up a boulder for a better view. Suddenly, something hit his thigh. A bullet had struck his sword. His leg was bruised, but the sword had saved him.

From atop the boulder, he could see a group of Confederate soldiers trying to sneak around the far left end of his line. If they succeeded, they would be able to attack from the rear.

Thinking quickly, Chamberlain spaced his soldiers farther apart. That stretched his line out to the left. Then he ordered the soldiers at the very end to drop back so their section formed an angle to the rest of the line.

Confederate troops charge up the rocky slopes of Little Round Top on July 2. The Rebels fought fiercely to try to capture the hill.

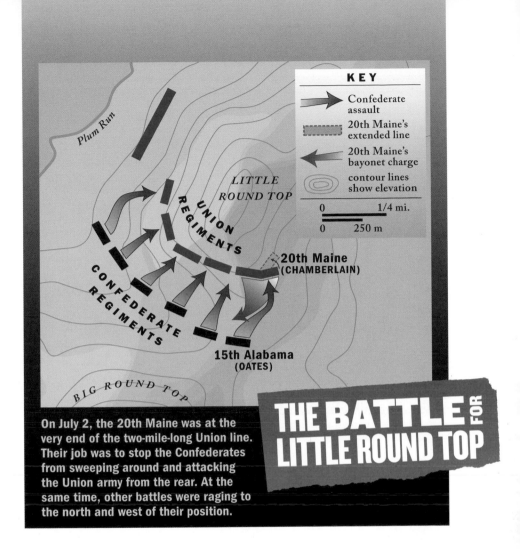

On July 2, the 20th Maine was at the very end of the two-mile-long Union line. Their job was to stop the Confederates from sweeping around and attacking the Union army from the rear. At the same time, other battles were raging to the north and west of their position.

THE BATTLE FOR LITTLE ROUND TOP

The Confederates charged, expecting to find Chamberlain's flank unprotected. Instead, they ran into a wall of Union troops. Once again, the Maine men had held off the Alabamians.

Hand-to-Hand Combat

As daylight faded, the Confederates fought desperately to take Little Round Top.

The 20th Maine fought just as fiercely to hold it. "The edge of the conflict swayed to and fro, with wild whirlpools and eddies," Chamberlain later recalled. "At times, I saw around me more of the enemy than of my own men."

This painting shows Colonel Chamberlain (at center, with sword) leading a desperate bayonet charge against Rebel soldiers trying to capture Little Round Top.

Curses, sobs, and screams of pain filled the air. All over the slopes of Little Round Top, men were dying.

Five times, the Rebels gained ground. "Squads of the enemy broke through our line," Chamberlain remembered, "and the fighting was literally hand-to-hand." Five times, the Maine men pushed back into position.

Chamberlain could hear his soldiers calling out for more ammunition. He ordered them to search the bodies of the dead and wounded for unspent rounds.

A Civil War ammunition canister

Soon, Chamberlain's men were down to their last bullets. He didn't think they could hold off another attack.

"A critical moment has arrived," one Maine soldier remembered thinking. "We must advance or retreat. It must not be the latter, but how can it be the former?"

Chamberlain made a daring decision. The 20th Maine would attack. It was a desperate gamble, but as he said later, "There was nothing [to do] but to take the offensive." His men would have the advantage of moving downhill, as well as the element of surprise, in their favor.

With the Rebels just 30 yards away, Chamberlain ordered the attack. "Bayonets!" he yelled.

The order "caught fire and swept along the ranks," as he later described it. "Bayonets!" the men called to each other. They quickly snapped the blades into place. Then, holding their rifles low, they charged.

"The Blood Stood in Puddles"

Yelling and cursing, the Maine men roared down the hill.

The exhausted Confederates were taken completely by surprise. Some tried to make a stand, but the thrusting bayonets cut them down. Others took off as fast as they could, tripping over bodies as they ran. "The dead literally covered the ground," Colonel Oates wrote later. "The blood stood in puddles."

A Confederate officer brandishing a sword and a pistol took a shot at Chamberlain—and missed. Then he handed over his weapons. Many other Rebels also surrendered.

The battle was over. The men of the 20th Maine had held Little Round Top—but at a terrible price. At least 40 of Chamberlain's men had been killed, and another 90 were badly wounded. Chamberlain would later learn that his commander, Colonel Vincent, had been mortally wounded on another part of the hill.

TERRIBLE LOSSES

About 150 of Colonel Oates's men had been wounded or killed, and about 90 were taken prisoner. One of the casualties was Oates's brother. "My beloved brother was pierced through with eight bullets and fell mortally wounded," the colonel wrote. But the losses at Little Round Top were just a fraction of the total casualties on July 2. About 9,000 soldiers in each army had been wounded or killed.

At the end of the day, the Union troops still held the high ground, thanks in no small part to the 20th Maine's defense of Little Round Top.

Lee's relentless attacks had gained him little. But as Chamberlain's men slept on the battlefield that night, the Confederate general was already planning his next move.

A Confederate sharpshooter lies dead
near the foot of Little Round Top.

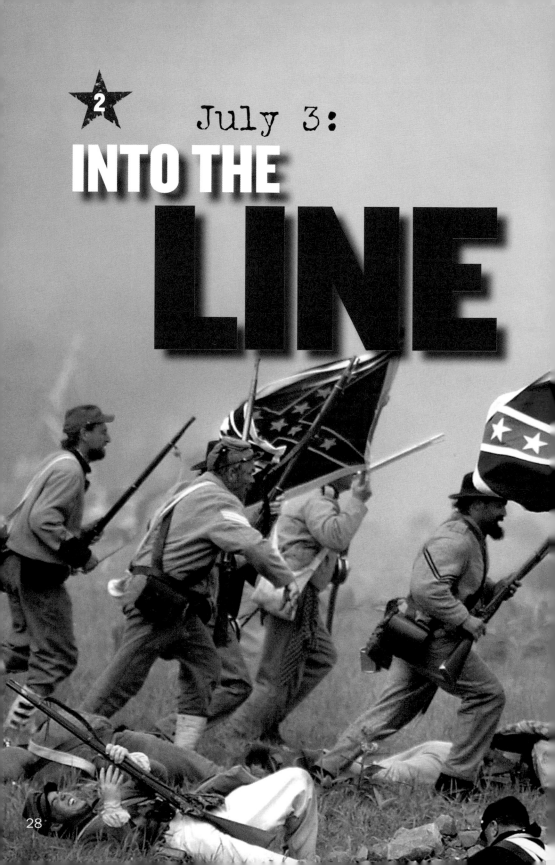

2 July 3:
INTO THE
LINE

Every year, Civil War fans act out key events of the war. This 2003 photo shows a re-enactment of Pickett's Charge, the Rebels' massive assault on the Union line on July 3, 1863.

OF FIRE

Confederate General Robert E. Lee's attacks on July 2 had failed. But now he had a new plan. Was it brilliant—or suicidal?

General Robert E. Lee was running out of time. Over the past two days, the Army of Northern Virginia had taken a terrible beating. Lee didn't have enough troops left to continue fighting much longer. The battle would be won or lost on this hot day.

With his most trusted commander, General James Longstreet, at his side, Lee rode out to survey the Union line. The two men gazed across a mile of open fields at Cemetery Ridge, where thousands of Union troops were firmly dug in.

Lee considered his alternatives. His repeated attacks on the Union flanks had failed, but what if he attacked the very center of the Union line? He doubted that Union General George Meade would be expecting such a bold move.

Lee turned to Longstreet and announced his decision: Longstreet would lead 13,000 soldiers from three divisions on a frontal assault. Longstreet was shocked. To reach the Union line, his troops would have to cross a wide stretch of open fields. They would make an easy target for Union cannons and rifles on Cemetery Ridge. It seemed like a suicidal plan.

To reach the Union line, Lee's troops would have to cross these open fields. The terrain offered no protection from enemy fire.

"General Lee," Longstreet protested, "there never was a body of [13,000] men who could make that attack successfully." Instead, Longstreet said, they should dig in and wait for Meade to attack *them*.

But Lee insisted. He believed that the Union line's weakest point was at its center. It looked as though there were fewer troops there than on the heavily defended flanks. And those troops were on lower ground than the soldiers on the hills, with only a low stone wall for protection.

If Lee's men could smash through at the center, they would split the Union army in half— and send the pieces flying. "The enemy is *there*, General Longstreet," Lee said, pointing across the fields, "and I am going to strike him."

General Longstreet gives orders to an officer during the battle.

A Massive Barrage

General Longstreet was sure that his troops were doomed.

Longstreet believed that Lee was making a terrible mistake. But he had to execute his orders. He found his top commanders and explained Lee's plan. He chose General George Pickett and two other officers to lead the attack.

Pickett was excited. His division of Virginia men hadn't seen any action at Gettysburg. They were eager to prove themselves.

By late morning, Longstreet had all three divisions in formation, waiting to move out. But it would be hours before they would begin their long trek across the fields. Lee had ordered the attack to begin with a massive artillery assault.

Lee hoped the artillery barrage would accomplish two things. First, he wanted to wipe out the Union cannons to prevent them from firing on Pickett's men as they advanced across the open field. Second, Lee hoped to wound or kill as many Union infantrymen as possible before the Rebels attacked the Union line.

At 1:00 P.M., 140 Confederate cannons started blasting away at the Union line. As shells ripped through the trees and exploded around them, Union artillerymen scrambled to fire back. Soon the battlefield was shaking with thunderous explosions.

One Confederate officer later described the massive barrage: "Looking up the valley towards Gettysburg, the hills on either side were capped with crowns of flame and smoke, as [hundreds of cannons] vomited their iron hail upon each other."

But unknown to Lee, his artillery assault was failing. Many shells were flying right over the Union line; others didn't even explode. As a result, the Union lost only a few infantrymen.

A Union artillery crew fires on a Confederate position.

This 1863 newspaper illustration shows Union cannons at Gettysburg firing across a wide field at Confederate artillery positions.

The bombardment continued for over an hour. Then suddenly, the Union cannons stopped firing. Having used up most of their ammunition, the Rebels ceased firing as well. They assumed that the Union artillery had been badly damaged or had run out of ammo. But in fact, Meade had guessed that Lee was planning a direct assault on his line. The Union artillery teams were now saving their ammo to repel that attack.

As the cannons fell silent, Pickett turned to Longstreet. Was it time to advance? Longstreet looked out at the Rebel troops. When he gave the order to march, he would be sending thousands of young men to their deaths. The general felt too upset to speak. He turned to Pickett and nodded.

Confederate General George E. Pickett

MILITARY SPEAK

How many *regiments* in a *brigade*? Here's a breakdown of military units during the Civil War.

UNIT	LEADER	SIZE	FYI
COMPANY	captain and 2 lieutenants	100 soldiers	Companies were recruited in towns or counties.
REGIMENT	colonel	1,000 soldiers (10 companies)	Regiments were identified by number and state: the 20th Maine, for example.
BRIGADE	brigadier general	3,000–5,000 soldiers (3–5 regiments)	A brigade's effectiveness depended on how well its regiments worked together.
DIVISION	brigadier general	12,000–25,000 soldiers (4–5 brigades)	Divisions were often named for their commanders.
CORPS	lieutenant general (Confederacy) major general (Union)	24,000 or more soldiers (2 or more divisions)	Units from seven Union corps fought at the Battle of Gettysburg.
ARMY	full general (Confederacy) major general (Union)	several corps	Confederate armies were often named for regions: the Army of Northern Virginia, for example.

THE BIG GUNS

During most Civil War battles, both sides brought out the big guns—the artillery.

Battles often began with an artillery barrage—a massive bombardment intended to soften the enemy's forces before an infantry charge began.

The cannons were operated by teams of up to eight men. Some guns could hit targets that were almost two miles away. Cannons designed for short-range use inflicted great damage on enemy troops within 400 yards.

Long-range cannons hurled solid cannonballs at buildings, fortified positions, and large groups of soldiers. They also fired hollow shells filled with gunpowder that were timed to explode after impact. Short-range guns fired canisters—cans packed with metal balls that sprayed deadly shrapnel in all directions.

Teams of four to six horses were used to pull the cannons into position. These teams were often targeted by the enemy. Without horses, the cannons could not be moved.

A Civil War cannon at Gettysburg. Today, the battlefield is a national park that attracts about two million visitors a year.

Into the Line of Fire

"Up men and to your posts!" General Pickett shouted to the waiting troops. "Forward!"

Thirteen thousand men stepped out of the woods on Seminary Ridge and began to march across the fields. They were lined up in parade formation—in several orderly rows, one behind the next. The front row stretched almost a mile wide.

The Confederate troops advanced briskly under the hot July sun. On Cemetery Ridge, awed Union soldiers watched them approach. One Union officer said later, "[They moved] as with one soul, in perfect order . . . magnificent, grim, irresistible."

Suddenly, the Union cannons opened fire. The Rebels were stunned—they'd been certain that the Union artillery lay in ruins. But now Union shells were blasting huge holes in their ranks.

At times, as many as ten men were felled by a single shell. Screams of agony filled the smoky air.

The hot sun beat down on the surviving Rebels, making them

This illustration of Pickett's Charge was published in a newspaper of the day. Newspapers hired battlefield artists to observe and sketch battles.

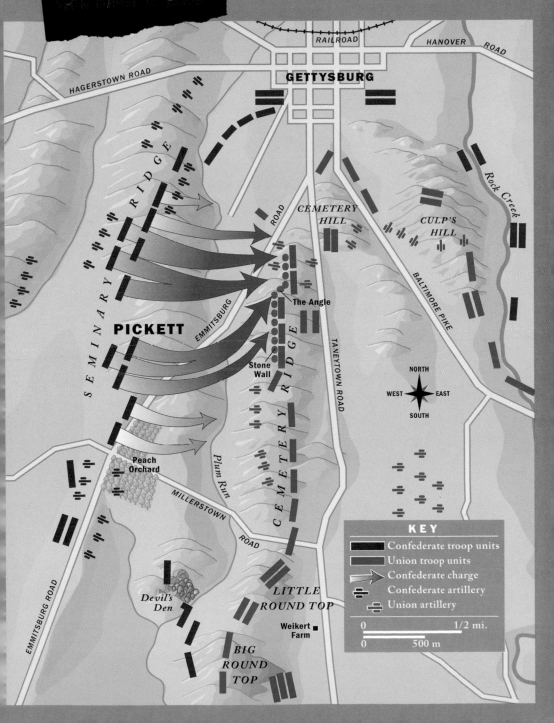

PICKETT'S CHARGE

On July 3, 13,000 Confederate troops led by General George Pickett attacked the center of the Union line. Some of the Confederates headed for the Angle, a bend in a stone wall that shielded Union troops.

RAILROAD

HANOVER ROAD

HAGERSTOWN ROAD

GETTYSBURG

Rock Creek

SEMINARY RIDGE

CEMETERY HILL

CULP'S HILL

BALTIMORE PIKE

The Angle

PICKETT

EMMITSBURG ROAD

Stone Wall

CEMETERY RIDGE

TANEYTOWN ROAD

NORTH

WEST · EAST

SOUTH

Peach Orchard

Plum Run

MILLERSTOWN ROAD

EMMITSBURG ROAD

Devil's Den

LITTLE ROUND TOP

Weikert Farm

BIG ROUND TOP

KEY

- Confederate troop units
- Union troop units
- Confederate charge
- Confederate artillery
- Union artillery

0 ———————— 1/2 mi.

0 ———————— 500 m

Confederate General Lewis A. Armistead (with hat on sword) and his men break through the Union line at the Angle.

sweat inside their heavy wool uniforms. The smoke from the cannons was so thick the troops could hardly see where they were going. Still, the Rebels marched on. As hundreds of men in the front line fell, others moved forward to fill the gaps. Soon, some were within 400 feet of the Union line.

A Confederate soldier's hat, left on the Gettysburg battlefield

Now the Rebels were in range of the Union rifles. Infantrymen behind the stone wall opened up on Pickett's men. Many bullets found their targets, and everywhere men were falling, dead or dying.

The Confederates kept coming, firing as they advanced. General Pickett watched in horror as the men in his division were struck down by the hundreds. But he continued to urge the survivors on.

"I never saw troops behave more magnificently than Pickett's division of Virginians did today in that grand charge upon the enemy," General Lee would say later.

Storming the Wall
Against all odds, some soldiers in Pickett's division were nearing the Union line.

Led by General Lewis A. Armistead, about 300 soldiers from Virginia surged forward toward the low stone wall that shielded many Union defenders.

Facing the Virginians were soldiers of the 71st Pennsylvania Regiment. They were dug in behind a bend in the wall that would become known as "the Angle." Nearby, a Union artillery team manned two cannons.

With his hat dangling from his sword, Armistead urged his men forward. They raced for the wall, shooting their guns and screaming. When the Pennsylvanians saw the swarms of Rebels coming toward them, they quickly retreated.

Two Confederate soldiers lie dead on the battlefield at Gettysburg.

The Virginians reached the wall and leaped over it, storming through the gap in the line. Armistead ran forward to try to capture the cannons. He had just reached them when he was shot. He fell, mortally wounded.

Two Union regiments hurried to close the gap in their line. Fierce close-up fighting broke out. Men fired into each other's faces. They stabbed each other with bayonets and swords. All around, men were falling "legless, armless, headless," as one survivor put it, and there were "ghastly heaps of dead men."

Every southerner who jumped over the wall was captured or killed. And no other Rebels reached the Union line. Pickett's Charge, as it came to be called, was over. Those Rebels who survived surrendered or fled back to the rear.

General Lee watched his troops retreat. He knew that the charge had been a catastrophic mistake—one he would regret for the rest of his life. Still, he tried to rally his men. They had to be ready for a possible counterattack by the Union army.

Lee found Pickett and urged him to prepare his division for more fighting. Pickett could not believe his ears. "General," he replied bitterly, "I have no division now."

Some 5,600 Rebels had been killed, injured, or captured during the one-hour assault. About 2,800 of those men came from Pickett's division alone.

Fields Soaked in Blood
Pickett's Charge brought the fighting at Gettysburg to a bloody end.

During the three days of battle, 23,000 Union soldiers and 28,000 Confederates had been killed, wounded, or taken prisoner.

In the wake of Pickett's Charge, Lee was forced to order the Army of Northern Virginia to retreat. They would never cross into Union territory again.

They left behind a battlefield still strewn with the bloodied and bloated corpses of thousands of soldiers and horses. There were bodies everywhere—in the fields and orchards, on the slopes of the nearby hills, under the trees in the woods.

Thousands of wounded soldiers had been left behind. The people of Gettysburg would spend many months nursing them back to health.

Pickett, who had longed for glory, was left with haunting memories of the soldiers who had followed him into battle. "The moans of my wounded boys, the sight of the dead, upturned faces, flood my soul with grief," he wrote to his wife. "And here am I whom they trusted, whom they followed, leaving them on that field of carnage . . ."

On July 4, Lee's Confederate army retreated. The procession of soldiers stretched for miles.

41

3

The bodies of horses killed in the battle surround a Gettysburg farmhouse.

July 1-3: "THE REBELS ARE COMING!"

Tillie Pierce was a carefree teenager growing up in Gettysburg. Then she was thrust into the middle of a bloody battle.

The Rebels are coming! The Rebels are coming!" The news spread like wildfire through Gettysburg, Pennsylvania. It soon reached the quiet classroom where Tillie Pierce, 15, and her classmates were studying.

"Children, run home!" the teacher ordered.

For the first two years of the Civil War, most of the battles had taken place in the South. Tillie never imagined that the violence would threaten her peaceful little town.

Then, in June 1863, Confederate General Robert E. Lee led his army north, into Pennsylvania. The troops were running low on supplies, so they raided the towns they passed through. "We often heard of their taking horses and cattle, carrying off property and destroying buildings," Tillie remembered.

The townspeople were terrified. As Tillie later wrote, "They had none of the weapons or munitions of war. They were not drilled and were totally unprepared. . . . They were civilians."

Some of the older men gathered whatever weapons they could find—"old rusty swords and guns, pitch-forks, shovels, and pick-axes"—to prepare to defend their town.

Many free blacks fled Gettysburg because they "regarded the Rebels as having an especial hatred toward them." Their fears were well-founded. Raiders from Virginia, a slave state,

In this drawing from 1863, citizens of York, Pennsylvania, watch as Confederate soldiers march through town, headed for Gettysburg.

were known to travel north in search of escaped slaves—and even to kidnap free blacks and sell them into slavery.

On June 26, the townspeople's fears were realized when a Rebel raiding party rode into Gettysburg. Firing pistols into the air, the men looted stores and homes for supplies.

Then the raiders left as suddenly as they had arrived, taking Tillie's horse with them. "I felt that I had been robbed of a dear friend," she wrote.

The Confederates would return soon. And this time, they would bring war.

The Wounded and Dying

Tillie heard the loud roar of cannons outside of town. Clouds of smoke rose above Seminary Ridge.

At dawn on July 1, advance troops from the Union and Confederate armies had clashed just northwest of Gettysburg. Reinforcements were now rushing toward the fighting. "The battle was waging," Tillie realized.

The Battle of Gettysburg had begun—and Tillie's parents quickly arranged to get her out of town. Tillie would join a neighbor, Mrs. Schriver, who was taking her children to her parents' home, three miles south of Gettysburg.

The small band set off down Taneytown Road, one of the main roads out of Gettysburg. As they walked, they could see the battle raging on Seminary Ridge. There were "troops moving hither and thither," Tillie wrote later. She saw "the smoke of the conflict arising from the fields, shells bursting in the air."

The group made slow progress. Taneytown Road was muddy and full of deep ruts. It had been torn up by the heavy traffic of Union soldiers, horses, wagons, and cannons. But at last, Tillie and the others reached the home of Mrs. Schriver's parents—the Weikert farm.

That afternoon, Confederate troops had pushed Union troops south, through Gettysburg and onto the slopes of Culp's Hill and Cemetery Hill. The fighting had been brutal, and the Union army had suffered terrible losses.

Tillie Pierce as a teenager

A road out of Gettysburg. This photo is from the 1860s.

Soon after Tillie arrived at the Weikerts', wounded Union soldiers began appearing at the door, asking for shelter and medical aid. They kept coming for hours, Tillie recalled, "some limping, some with their heads and arms in bandages, some crawling, others carried on stretchers."

By evening, the Weikerts' barn was filled with injured and dying soldiers. Tillie and another girl went to find out how they could help—but the sight of so many suffering soldiers horrified them. They ran back to the house, sobbing.

"Nothing before in my experience has ever paralleled the sight we then and there beheld," Tillie wrote.

But worse was yet to come.

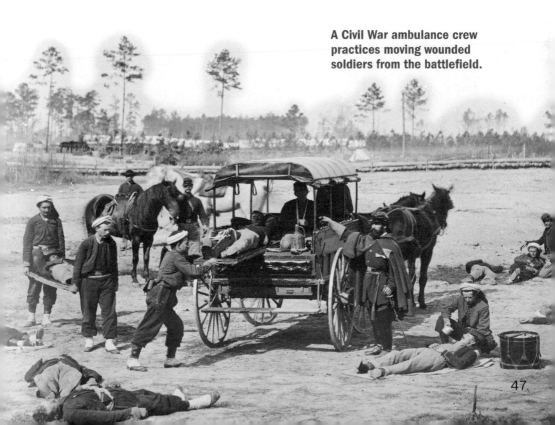
A Civil War ambulance crew practices moving wounded soldiers from the battlefield.

47

In this 1995 re-enactment at Gettysburg, Confederate troops (in the foreground) advance on a well-defended Union position.

JULY 1–3: "THE REBELS ARE COMING!"

"We Were All Terror-Stricken"

The second day of battle dawned, cloudy and warm.

Thousands of Union troops passed the farm that morning, headed into battle. Tillie hurried back and forth from a spring to bring water to the hot, thirsty soldiers.

Union troops had been arriving all night. General George Gordon Meade had ordered them to dig in along Cemetery Ridge. Now 95,000 Union soldiers were preparing to battle 75,000 Rebels. The two armies faced each other in long lines stretching for several miles south of town.

The fighting began later that afternoon and raged for hours in the fields and hills around Gettysburg. One of the fiercest battles took place on Little Round Top, a hill just behind the Weikert house.

The sounds of the battle were so "terrible and severe" that Tillie and the Weikerts could barely hear themselves speak. At times shells would come "flying over Round Top and explode high in the air"—right above the Weikert house.

"We were all terror-stricken and hardly knew what to do," Tillie recalled.

As the day went on, many more wounded Union soldiers came to the Weikert farmhouse. "The orchard and space around the buildings were covered with the shattered and dying, and the barn became more and more crowded," Tillie wrote.

Tillie struggled to control her feelings and force herself to help. "I made myself useful in doing whatever I could to assist the surgeons and nurses."

Later that night, Tillie tended a badly injured soldier

Body armor worn by a Union soldier at Gettysburg

in the farmhouse basement. He asked her to return the next morning, and she readily agreed.

"Now don't forget your promise," he said as she left.

"No indeed," Tillie answered.

"An Awful Sacrifice"

On the third day of the battle, Tillie woke up worrying about the wounded soldier.

She hurried downstairs, where a friend sat beside the man Tillie had nursed the night before. The soldier's body was still. He had died during the night.

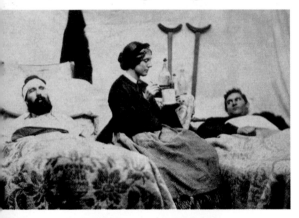

Ann Bell, a nurse, tends to two Union soldiers. Her skill made her "worth more to the Union army than many of us generals," said one commander.

"I had kept my promise," she later recalled sorrowfully, "but he was not there to greet me."

Tillie had little time to absorb the shock. The Weikerts told her that they needed to flee to a safer place. Union soldiers had warned them that the fighting might come dangerously close to their house that day.

Hours later, after the raging battle died down, Tillie and the others returned to the Weikert farm. There were wounded and dying soldiers as far as the eye could see. "I fairly shrank back aghast at the awful sight presented. . . . The air was filled with moanings, and groanings." She had to walk carefully to avoid stepping on dead bodies.

When she entered the house, Tillie saw surgeons sawing off soldiers' shattered arms and legs. And through the window, she could see "a pile of limbs reaching higher than the fence."

Finally, the horrifying day drew to a close. Tillie heard Union

A surgeon performs an amputation at a field hospital in Gettysburg.

soldiers saying that Confederate General George Pickett had led a doomed charge against the center of the Union line. They said that the Rebels had been whipped.

But the Union victory, Tillie reflected, had come at a terrible cost—"an awful sacrifice" of young lives.

The amputation kit of a Union surgeon; a bone from Union General Daniel Sickles's leg, which was amputated at Gettysburg; and the cannonball that hit Sickles.

The Folly of War

On July 7, Tillie headed home across the battlefield.

"The stench . . . was most sickening," she recalled. "Dead horses, swollen to almost twice their natural size, lay in all directions, stains of blood frequently met our gaze, and all kinds of army [equipment] covered the ground. Fences had disappeared, some buildings were gone, others ruined."

Confederate soldiers killed at Gettysburg lie in a mass grave.

It would be years before life in Gettysburg returned to normal. During the three days of battle, more than 7,500 soldiers had been killed. Tens of thousands more had been wounded. About 22,000 Union and Confederate soldiers, too badly injured to travel, had been left behind. It fell to Gettysburg's 2,400 residents to take care of them.

Tillie Pierce had witnessed the devastation firsthand. Like

A REUNION OF RIVALS

In July 1913, 50 years after the battle, more than 50,000 Civil War veterans attended a reunion in Gettysburg. Old soldiers from both sides wandered the battlefield together, trading war stories.

A highlight of the event was a reunion of Union and Confederate veterans of Pickett's Charge. The men shook hands across the stone wall where a few of Pickett's troops had briefly broken through the Union line.

Soon after the battle, the U.S. government set up Camp Letterman, a large tent hospital. Wounded soldiers from both the North and the South were treated here.

everyone else in the once-quiet little town, she was changed forever. And she hoped that others would never have to experience the horrors she had seen. "May the heart of this fair land be forever inclined unto wisdom," she wrote, "so that we may never fall into the folly of another war."

Two former adversaries shake hands at Gettysburg in 1913, 50 years after the battle.

A NEW BIRTH OF FREEDOM

I n November 1863, President Abraham Lincoln traveled to Gettysburg to deliver a speech dedicating a new Union cemetery.

The president looked out on the stray canteens, cups, shoes, and horse skeletons that still littered the fields. He told the audience of 15,000 that the soldiers buried at Gettysburg had died to defend their country. It was now up to "us the living," he said, to continue their "unfinished work," to keep fighting for "a new birth of freedom."

A few months later, Lincoln turned over command of the Union forces to Ulysses S. Grant. In May 1864, Grant launched a brutal six-week campaign that gradually forced Robert E. Lee's Confederate army back to Richmond, Virginia.

With Lee pinned down, Union General William Tecumseh Sherman led 100,000 troops into Georgia. He captured Atlanta in September, and by the end of the year his army had marched through Georgia

Lincoln delivers the Gettysburg Address.

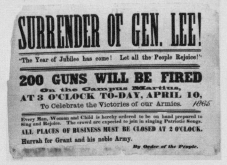

SURRENDER OF GEN. LEE!

"The Year of Jubilee has come! Let all the People Rejoice!"

200 GUNS WILL BE FIRED

On the Campus Martius,
AT 3 O'CLOCK TO-DAY, APRIL 10,
To Celebrate the Victories of our Armies. *1865*

Every Man, Woman and Child is hereby ordered to be on hand prepared to Sing and Rejoice. The crowd are expected to join in singing Patriotic Songs.
ALL PLACES OF BUSINESS MUST BE CLOSED AT 2 O'CLOCK.
Hurrah for Grant and his noble Army.

By Order of the People.

A northern newspaper announces the Confederate surrender.

to the port city of Savannah. He left behind a trail of twisted railroad lines, burned crops, and looted farms. "War is cruelty," Sherman observed.

The Confederacy lay in ruins. On April 9, 1865, Lee rode to a small town called Appomattox Court House and surrendered to Grant. After four years of fighting and more than 600,000 deaths, the war had come to an end.

Lincoln had only a few days to enjoy the peace. He was assassinated on April 14 by a Confederate sympathizer named John Wilkes Booth.

After the war, the 13th and 14th Amendments outlawed slavery and granted citizenship to African Americans. But for 3.5 million freed African Americans, short on resources and surrounded by their former enslavers, equality lay a long way off. It wasn't until a century later, during the civil rights movement, that the country truly experienced a "new birth of freedom."

Richmond, Virginia, after the war

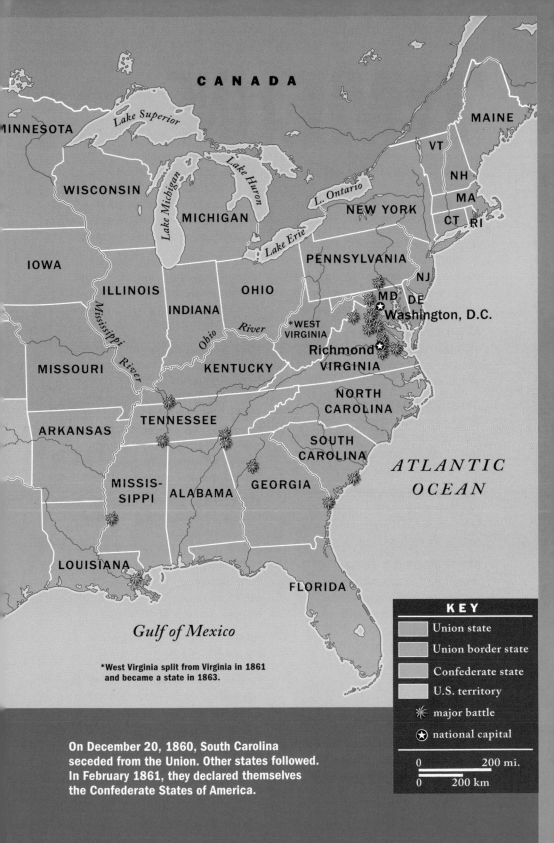

CANADA

MINNESOTA

Lake Superior

WISCONSIN

Lake Michigan

Lake Huron

MICHIGAN

L. Ontario

Lake Erie

NEW YORK

MAINE

VT

NH

MA

CT RI

IOWA

ILLINOIS

INDIANA

OHIO

PENNSYLVANIA

NJ

MD DE

Washington, D.C.

*WEST
VIRGINIA

Ohio   River

MISSOURI

KENTUCKY

Richmond

VIRGINIA

Mississippi River

ARKANSAS

TENNESSEE

NORTH
CAROLINA

MISSIS-
SIPPI

ALABAMA

GEORGIA

SOUTH
CAROLINA

ATLANTIC
OCEAN

LOUISIANA

FLORIDA

Gulf of Mexico

*West Virginia split from Virginia in 1861
and became a state in 1863.

KEY

Union state

Union border state

Confederate state

U.S. territory

✳ major battle

★ national capital

0   200 mi.

0   200 km

On December 20, 1860, South Carolina
seceded from the Union. Other states followed.
In February 1861, they declared themselves
the Confederate States of America.

TIMELINE

APRIL 12, 1861: War begins when Confederate cannons fire on Fort Sumter, a Union fortress in Charleston Harbor, South Carolina.

JULY 18, 1861: 37,000 Union soldiers march on the Confederate capital at Richmond, Virginia. Three days later, they are routed by Confederates at Bull Run Creek.

APRIL 6–7, 1862: More than 100,000 soldiers fight at the Battle of Shiloh; 23,000 are wounded or killed.

APRIL 25, 1862: Ordered to blockade seaports and suffocate the Confederacy "like an anaconda," Union warships capture the port of New Orleans on April 25.

SEPTEMBER 17, 1862: General Lee marches north and invades Maryland, but General McClellan halts him at Antietam.

SEPTEMBER 22, 1862: President Lincoln issues the Emancipation Proclamation, declaring all African American people held in Confederate territory "forever free." (It is signed January 1, 1863.)

DECEMBER 13, 1862: Union troops are defeated by General Lee at the Battle of Fredericksburg.

MAY 1–4, 1863: Outnumbered almost 2 to 1, Lee defeats the Union army at Chancellorsville, Virginia.

JULY 4, 1863: The Union celebrates its victory at Gettysburg, as well as the surrender of the Confederate stronghold Vicksburg, Mississippi, after a 48-day siege.

JULY 13, 1863: Angry about the first military draft in U.S. history, a mob sparks a huge riot in New York City, attacking hundreds of African Americans.

JULY 18, 1863: The all-black 54th Massachusetts Volunteer Infantry Regiment loses almost half its men during a failed attack on Fort Wagner in Charleston, South Carolina. The regiment's courage under fire inspires thousands of African Americans to join the Union army.

MARCH 12, 1864: President Lincoln gives General U.S. Grant command of the entire Union military. Grant sets out to destroy Lee's Army of Northern Virginia. After suffering nearly 100,000 combined casualties, the two armies reach a stalemate.

APRIL 3, 1865: Union troops capture Richmond, Virginia.

APRIL 9, 1865: General Lee surrenders to General Grant at Appomattox Court House.

APRIL 14, 1865: President Lincoln is assassinated.

RESOURCES

BOOKS

Burgan, Michael. *The Battle of Gettysburg (Graphic History)*. Mankato, MN: Capstone Press, 2006.

Elish, Dan. *The Battle of Gettysburg (Cornerstones of Freedom, Second Series)*. New York: Children's Press, 2008.

Ford, Carin T. *The Battle of Gettysburg and Lincoln's Gettysburg Address*. Berkeley Heights, NJ: Enslow Publishers, 2004.

January, Brendan. *Gettysburg: July 1–3, 1863 (American Battlefields)*. New York: Enchanted Lion Books, 2004.

Murphy, Jim. *The Long Road to Gettysburg*. New York: Clarion Books, 1992.

Olson, Kay M. *The Gettysburg Address in Translation: What It Really Means*. Mankato MN: Capstone Press, 2009.

WEBSITES

The Civil War
www.pbs.org/civilwar

This is the online companion to the highly acclaimed PBS series *The Civil War*. Includes historical photographs, maps, and biographies.

The Gettysburg Address
www.loc.gov/exhibits/gadd

This Library of Congress online exhibition includes photographs of the handwritten Gettysburg Address, as well as the only known photograph of Abraham Lincoln at Gettysburg.

The Gettysburg Foundation
www.gettysburgfoundation.org

This site provides a wealth of information about the Battle of Gettysburg.

Gettysburg National Military Park
www.nps.gov/gett

This site, sponsored by the National Park Service, includes a "virtual tour" with an in-depth look at each day of battle.

DICTIONARY

A

abolish (uh-BOL-ish) *verb* to officially put an end to something

artillery (ar-TIL-uh-ree) *noun* large, crew-operated guns such as cannons

assassinate (uh-SASS-uh-nate) *verb* to murder a well-known person, such as a president

B

barrage (buh-RAHZH) *noun* heavy artillery fire

bayonet (BAY-uh-net) *noun* a long blade that can be fastened to the end of a rifle

bloated (BLOH-tid) *adjective* swollen

bombardment (bom-BAHRD-muhnt) *noun* heavy and continuous artillery fire

C

canister (KAN-iss-tur) *noun* a can packed with small iron balls; when fired from a cannon, the can explodes and the balls scatter in all directions

carnage (KAR-nij) *noun* the slaughter of a large number of people

casualty (KAZH-oo-uhl-tee) *noun* someone who is injured, killed, or captured in a war

Confederacy (kuhn-FED-ur-uh-see) *noun* the 11 southern states that seceded from the rest of the United States just before the Civil War

Confederate (kuhn-FED-ur-uht) *adjective* having to do with the Confederacy

D

devastation (dev-uh-STAY-shun) *noun* horrible damage and destruction

E

Emancipation Proclamation (i-man-si-PAY-shun prak-luh-MAY-shun) *noun* the executive order issued by President Lincoln in September 1862 declaring the freedom of all slaves held in Confederate territory

enlist (en-LIST) *verb* to join or get someone to join the armed forces

F

flank (FLANGK) *noun* the far left or right side of a group of soldiers

folly (FOL-ee) *noun* foolishness

I

infantry (IN-fuhn-tree) *noun* the part of the army that fights on foot

M

mortally (MOR-tuhl-ee) *adverb* in a manner that causes death

munitions (myoo-NISH-uhns) *noun* military weapons, ammunition, and equipment

R

Rebel (REB-uhl) *noun* slang term for a Confederate soldier

reinforcements (ree-in-FORSS-muhnts) *noun* extra troops sent in to strengthen a fighting force

S

secede (si-SEED) *verb* to formally break away or withdraw from a group, organization, or country

shell (SHEL) *noun* a type of small bomb that is fired from a cannon

smoothbore musket (SMOOTH-bor MUHS-kit) *noun* a gun with a smooth barrel rather than a barrel with spiraled grooves

U

Union (YOON-yun) *noun* during the Civil War, the states that remained loyal to the federal government of the United States

Y

Yankee (YANG-kee) *noun* slang term for a Union soldier or a northerner

INDEX

ABOUT THIS BOOK

Often, when we study historical events, the focus is mostly on the big, well-known stories. While researching this book, I realized that the Civil War is also a source of fascinating true stories about ordinary people. Millions of average American citizens lived through the Civil War, and for most, it was a life-changing event.

Until the Civil War broke out, Joshua Chamberlain led a quiet life as a college professor. He had never served as a soldier, and probably never expected to fight in a war. But he became a hero at Gettysburg, and that changed his life. He went on to be elected governor of Maine—mostly on the strength of his reputation as a war hero.

Tillie Pierce was just an ordinary teenager when the war came to her hometown. But by the time the Battle of Gettysburg ended, she had seen and done things most teenagers would not experience in their whole lives. Later, she wrote a memoir describing the horrors of war from a personal perspective, instead of from the usual military point of view.

To do your own research on the Civil War, you might want to start with the Internet. A search engine can lead you to hundreds of sites dealing with every aspect of the war. Your school or public library is also a great place to look. You'll find shelves of nonfiction history books, historical novels, and photo collections about the Civil War.

The following books were useful in writing this book:

Alleman, Tillie Pierce. *At Gettysburg: Or, What a Girl Saw and Heard of the Battle. A True Narrative.* New York: W. Lake Borland, 1889. http://digital.library.upenn.edu/women/alleman/gettysburg/gettysburg.html

McPherson, James. *Fields of Fury: The American Civil War.* New York: Simon and Schuster Children's Publishing Division, 2002.

Shaara, Michael. *The Killer Angels.* New York: Ballantine Books, 1974.

Ward, Geoffrey C., with Ric Burns and Ken Burns. *The Civil War: An Illustrated History.* New York: Alfred A. Knopf, 1994.

—Jennifer Johnson